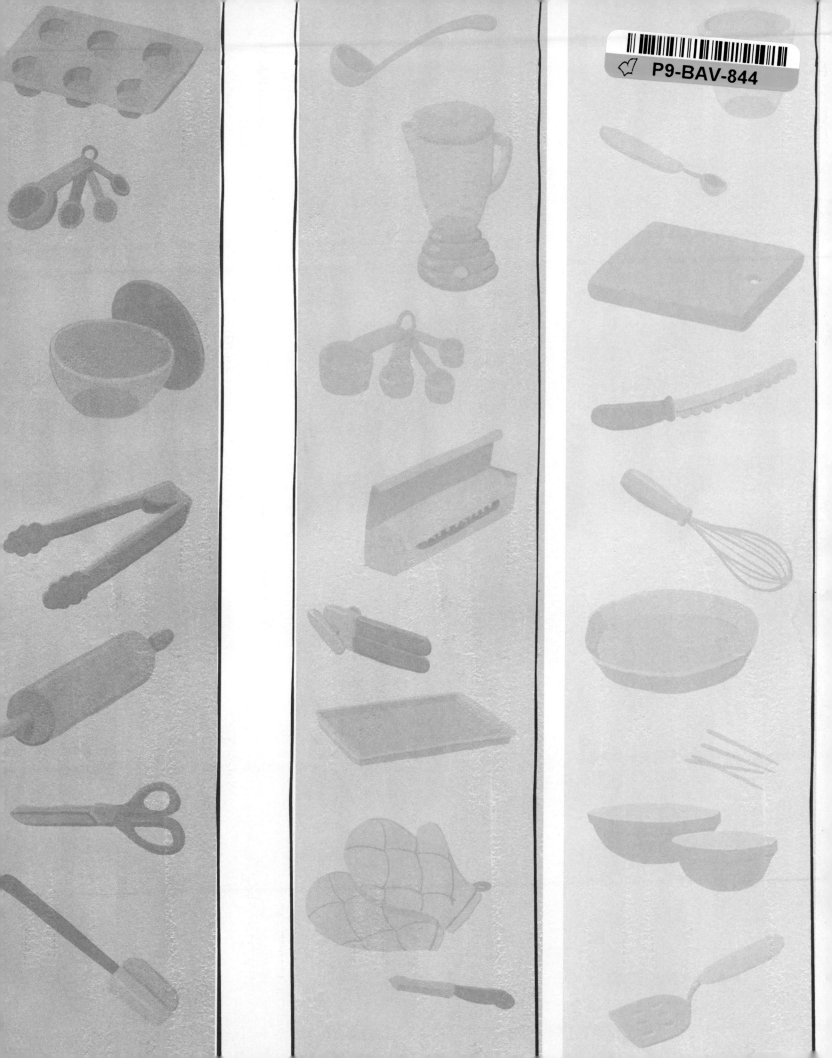

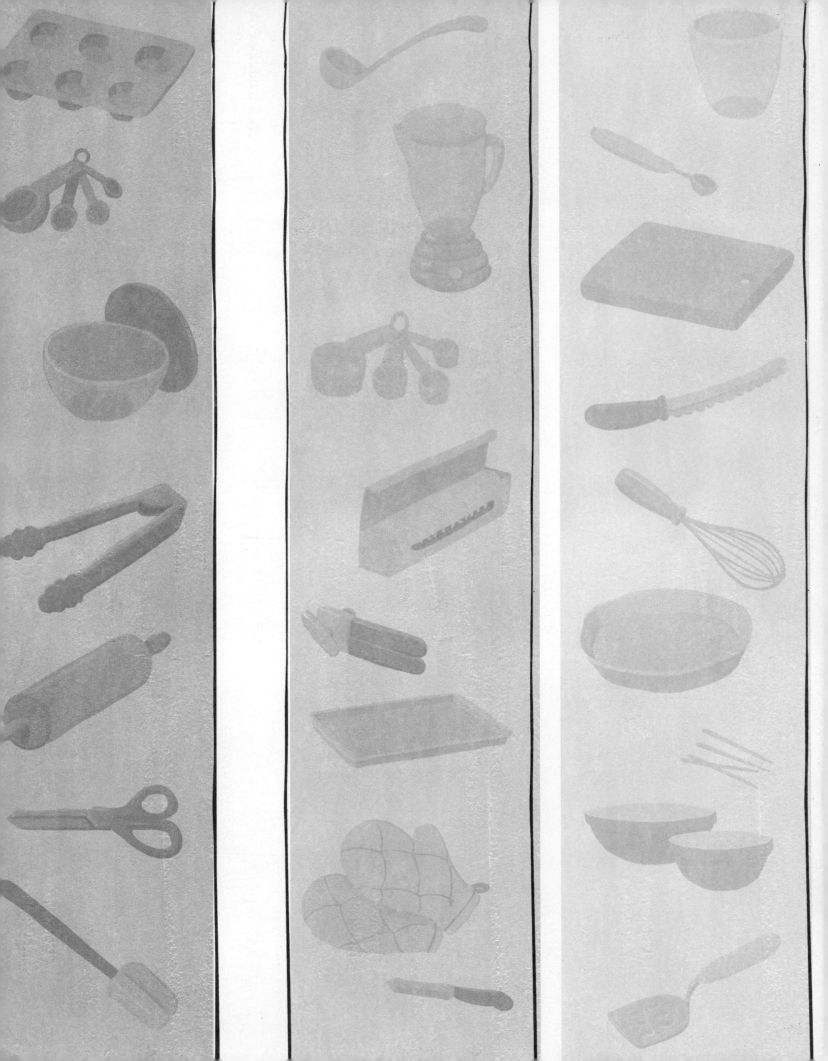

Indoor S'mores

and Other Tasty Treats for Special Occasions

by Nick Fauchald   illustrated by Rick Peterson

Special thanks to our content adviser:
Joanne L. Slavin, Ph.D., R.D.
Professor of Food Science and Nutrition
University of Minnesota

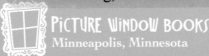

PICTURE WINDOW BOOKS
Minneapolis, Minnesota

Editors: Christianne Jones and Carol Jones
Designer: Tracy Davies
Page Production: Melissa Kes

Art Director: Nathan Gassman
The illustrations in this book were created with acrylics and gouache.

Picture Window Books • 151 Good Counsel Drive • P.O. Box 669 • Mankato, MN 56002-0669
877-845-8392 • www.picturewindowbooks.com

The illustration on page 5 is from *www.mypyramid.gov.*

Printed in the United States of America
All books published by Picture Window Books are manufactured
with paper containing at least 10 percent post-consumer waste.

Library of Congress Cataloging-in-Publication Data
Fauchald, Nick.
Indoor s'mores : and other tasty treats for special occasions / by Nick Fauchald ; illustrated by Rick Peterson.
p. cm. — (Kids dish)
Includes index.
ISBN-13: 978-1-4048-4000-3 (library binding)
1. Cookery—Juvenile literature. 2. Snack food—Juvenile literature. I. Peterson, Rick. II. Title.
TX652.5.F394 2008
641.5—dc22   2007032922

Editors' note: The author based the difficulty levels of the recipes on the skills and time required, as well
as the number of ingredients and tools needed. Adult help and supervision is required for all recipes.

Table of Contents

EASY

INTERMEDIATE

ADVANCED

Nick Fauchald is the author of many children's books. After attending the French Culinary School in Manhattan, he helped launch the magazine *Every Day with Rachael Ray*. He is currently an editor at *Food & Wine* magazine and lives in New York City. Although Nick has worked with some of the world's best chefs, he still thinks kids are the most fun and creative cooks to work with.

Dear Kids,

One of the best ways to celebrate a special occasion is by making something delicious to serve. This cookbook is full of ways to turn food into a party, and the recipes can be made with only a little help from an adult.

Cooking is fun, and safety in the kitchen is very important. As you begin your cooking adventure, please remember these tips:

★ Make sure an adult is in the kitchen with you.
★ Tie back your hair and tuck in all loose clothing.
★ Read the recipe from start to finish before you begin.
★ Wash your hands before you start and whenever they get messy.
★ Wash all fresh fruits and vegetables.
★ Take your time cutting the ingredients.
★ Use oven mitts whenever you are working with hot foods or equipment.
★ Stay in the kitchen the entire time you are cooking.
★ Clean up when you are finished.

Now, choose a recipe that sounds tasty, check with an adult, and get cooking. Your friends and family are hungry!

Enjoy,
Nick

Note to Adults:

Learning to cook is an exciting, challenging adventure for young people. It helps kids build confidence, learn responsibility, become familiar with food and nutrition, practice math, science, and motor skills, and follow directions. Here are some ways you can help kids get the most out of their cooking experiences:

• Encourage them to read the entire recipe before they begin cooking. Make sure they have everything they need and understand all of the steps.

• Make sure young cooks have a kid-friendly workspace. If your kitchen counter is too high for them, offer them a step stool or a table to work at.

• Expect new cooks to make a little mess, and encourage them to clean it up when they are finished.

• Help multiple cooks divide the tasks before they begin.

• Enjoy what the kids just cooked together.

MyPyramid

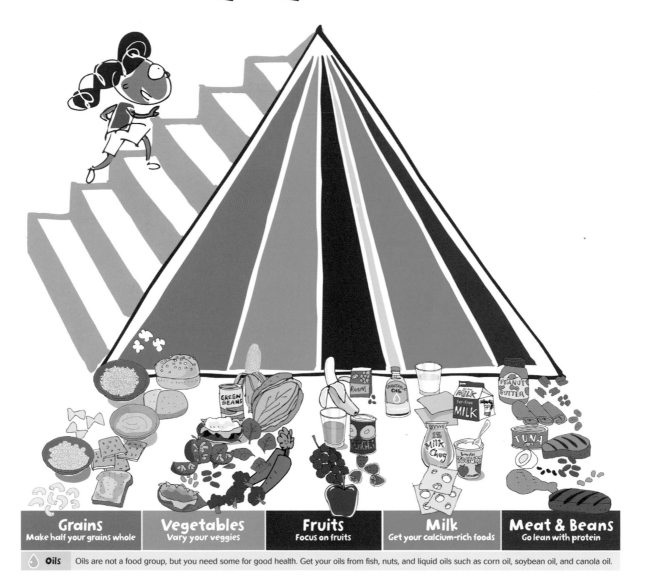

In 2005, the U.S. government created MyPyramid, a plan for healthy eating and living. The new MyPyramid plan contains 12 separate diet plans based on your age, gender, and activity level. For more information about MyPyramid, visit *www.mypyramid.gov.*

The pyramid at the top of each recipe shows the main food groups included. Use the index to find recipes that include food from the food group of your choice, major ingredients used, recipe levels, and appliances/equipment needed.

Special Tips and Glossary

Cracking Eggs: Tap the egg on the counter until it cracks. Hold the egg over a small bowl. Gently pull the two halves of the shell apart until the egg falls into the bowl.

Measuring Dry Ingredients: Measure dry ingredients (such as flour and sugar) by spooning the ingredient into a measuring cup until it's full. Then level off the top of the cup with the back of a butter knife.

Measuring Wet Ingredients: Place a clear measuring cup on a flat surface, then pour the liquid into the cup until it reaches the correct measuring line. Be sure to check the liquid at eye level.

Bake: cook food in an oven

Brush: spread a liquid or sauce with a pastry brush

Chop: cut food into small pieces of similar size

Cover: put container lid, plastic wrap, or aluminum foil over a food; use aluminum foil if you're baking the food, and plastic wrap if you're chilling, freezing, microwaving, or leaving it on the counter

Drain: pour off a liquid, leaving food behind; usually done with a strainer or colander

Grease: spread butter, cooking spray, or shortening on a piece of cookware so food doesn't stick

Juice: squeeze or use a citrus juicer to extract liquid from a fruit

Line: cover the bottom of a baking sheet or pan with foil or parchment paper

Melt: heat a solid (such as butter) until it becomes a liquid

Peel: remove the skin from a fruit or vegetable; be careful—peelers are sharp!

Preheat: turn an oven on before you use it; it usually takes about 15 minutes to preheat an oven

Slice: cut something into thin pieces

Spread: to make an even layer of something soft, like mayonnaise or frosting

Sprinkle: to scatter something in small bits

Stir: mix ingredients with a spoon until blended

Whisk: stir a mixture rapidly until it's smooth

METRIC CONVERSION CHART

1/8 teaspoon (0.5 milliliter)
1/4 teaspoon (1 milliliter)
1/2 teaspoon (2.5 milliliters)
1 teaspoon (5 milliliters)
1 1/2 teaspoons (7.5 milliliters)
4 teaspoons (20 milliliters)

1 tablespoon (15 milliliters)
2 tablespoons (30 milliliters)

1/4 cup (60 milliliters)
1/3 cup (75 milliliters)

1/2 cup (125 milliliters)
3/4 cup (180 milliliters)
1 cup (250 milliliters)
1 1/4 cups (300 milliliters)
1 1/2 cups (375 milliliters)
2 cups (500 milliliters)
3 cups (750 milliliters)
4 cups (1 liter)
4 1/2 cups (1 liter and 125 milliliters)
1 pint (0.5 liter)

1 ounce (28 grams)
1 1/2 ounces (42 grams)
3 ounces (84 grams)
12 ounces (336 grams)
14 ounces (392 grams)
16 1/2 ounces (462 grams)

TEMPERATURE CONVERSION CHART

325° Fahrenheit (165° Celsius)
350° Fahrenheit (175° Celsius)
375° Fahrenheit (190° Celsius)

Kitchen Tools

HERE ARE THE TOOLS YOU'LL USE WHEN COOKING THE RECIPES IN THIS BOOK★

8-by-8-inch baking pan

9-by-13-inch baking pan

Aluminum foil

Baking sheet

Butter knife

Can opener

Cocoa mugs

Cookie cutters

Cooling rack

Cooking spray

Cutting board

Citrus juicer

Drinking glass

Fork

Ice-cream scoop

Kitchen shears

Ladle

Measuring cups

Measuring spoons

Metal spatula

Microwave-safe bowls

Mixing bowls

Muffin cups

Pitcher

Muffin tin

Oven mitts

Paper towels

Parchment paper

Paring knife

Pastry brush

Plastic bags

Plastic wrap

Punch bowl

Rolling pin

Rubber spatula

Serrated knife

Spoon

Straws

Toothpicks

Whisk

Wooden spoon

Small, sharp knife

Vegetable peeler

Wooden skewers

This Recipe Includes **FRUITS**

Apple Party Punch

INGREDIENTS

1 orange
1 lemon
1 cup orange juice, chilled
4 cups apple juice, chilled
3 cups cranberry juice, chilled
2 cups ginger ale, chilled
1 pint rainbow sherbet

TOOLS

Serrated knife
Cutting board
Resealable plastic bags
Measuring cups
Large punch bowl
Wooden spoon
Ice-cream scoop
Ladle

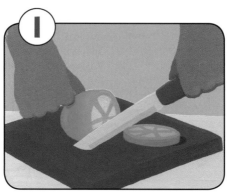

Ask an adult to cut the orange and lemon into slices.

Place the fruit slices in a resealable plastic bag and freeze for 1 hour or until ready to serve.

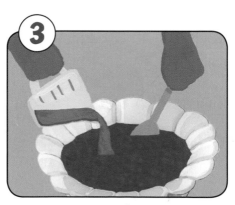

Pour the orange juice, apple juice, and cranberry juice into a large punch bowl and stir.

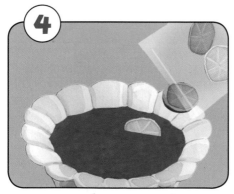

Add the frozen fruit slices and ginger ale.

8

NUTRITION NOTE★ Look for the word "unsweetened" on the label when buying juice for this vitamin-loaded punch. *Unsweetened* means "doesn't contain any added sugar."

5

Scoop sherbet into balls and place carefully in the punch.

6 Use a ladle to pour the punch into glasses.

FRUITS

This Recipe Includes

Lemonade Stand

INGREDIENTS
5 lemons
3 cups ice cubes
4 1/2 cups water
3/4 cup sugar

TOOLS
Serrated knife
Cutting board
Citrus juicer
Measuring cups
Large pitcher
Wooden spoon

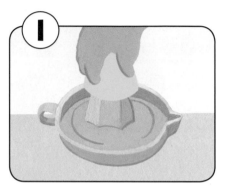

1 Ask an adult to cut four of the lemons in half. Use the citrus juicer to remove the juice from the lemon halves. Repeat with all of the lemons.

2 Put ice cubes into a large pitcher and pour the lemon juice over the ice.

3 Ask an adult to cut the remaining lemon into slices.

4 Add the water, lemon slices, and sugar to the lemon juice and stir until the sugar is dissolved.

5 Pour into glasses and serve.

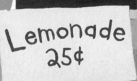

Lemonade 25¢

10

NUTRITION NOTE★
Lemons contain vitamin C, which can help your body fight illness.

Double Feature Popcorn

1

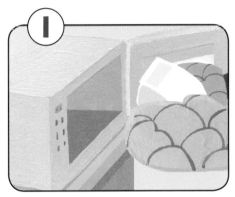

Ask an adult to prepare each bag of popcorn in the microwave according to package directions.

2

Add the Parmesan cheese and garlic salt to one bag, close, and shake well.

INGREDIENTS

Two 3-ounce bags plain
   microwave popcorn
1/4 cup freshly grated
   Parmesan cheese
1/2 teaspoon garlic salt
1 tablespoon sugar
1 teaspoon salt

TOOLS

Measuring spoons
Measuring cups

3

Add the sugar and salt to the remaining bag, close, and shake well.

 4 Pour into bowls and serve.

This Recipe Includes
MILK

Snowy Day Hot Chocolate

INGREDIENTS
3 cups milk
1/2 cup semisweet
   chocolate chips
1 tablespoon sugar
1/2 teaspoon ground
   cinnamon
1 large egg
Marshmallows for serving,
   optional

TOOLS
Measuring cups
Medium microwave-safe
   bowl
Measuring spoons
Wooden spoon
Small mixing bowl
Whisk
Oven mitts
4 cocoa mugs
Ladle

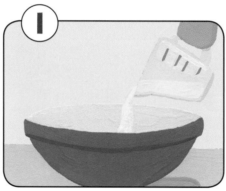

Pour the milk into a medium microwave-safe bowl. Ask an adult to heat the milk in the microwave for 2 minutes.

Add chocolate chips, sugar, and cinnamon to the milk and stir.

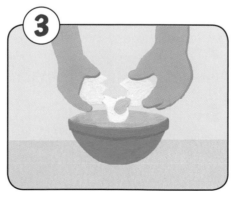

Break the egg into a small mixing bowl and whisk until smooth.

Add the egg to the chocolate mixture and whisk.

5

Ask an adult to heat the chocolate mixture in the microwave for 3 minutes. Whisk until smooth.

6 Use a ladle to pour the hot chocolate into four mugs. Serve with marshmallows, if desired.

This Recipe Includes
GRAINS

Indoor S'mores

INGREDIENTS

8 graham crackers
Two 1 1/2-ounce milk
    chocolate bars
8 large marshmallows

TOOLS

Baking sheet
Oven mitts

1 Preheat oven to 350°.

2 Break each graham cracker into two squares and place them on the baking sheet.

3 Break each chocolate bar into four pieces and place one square of chocolate on each cracker.

4 Place a marshmallow on each piece of chocolate.

5 Ask an adult to bake the s'mores in the oven for 5 minutes or until the marshmallows are softened and the chocolate begins to melt.

6 Top each s'more with a graham cracker square.

7 Serve.

14

Ice-Cream Soda Social

1

Pour 2 tablespoons of syrup into the bottom of each tall drinking glass.

2

Slowly pour in the seltzer water and stir until the foam fills the glass about two-thirds full.

3

Add 1 or 2 scoops of ice cream to the seltzer.

4 Drizzle 1 teaspoon chocolate syrup on top of each soda and serve with a straw and/or tall spoon.

INGREDIENTS

1/2 cup plus 4 teaspoons chocolate syrup
12-ounce bottle seltzer water
1 pint chocolate ice cream

TOOLS

4 tall drinking glasses
Measuring spoons
Measuring cups
Ice-cream scoop
Straws and/or tall spoon

15

This Recipe Includes
FRUITS

Campout Banana Boats

INGREDIENTS

4 bananas
1/4 cup mini marshmallows
1/4 cup chocolate chips
4 teaspoons brown sugar

TOOLS

Butter knife
Cutting board
Measuring cups
Measuring spoons
Four 12-inch squares of
    aluminum foil
Baking sheet
Oven mitts

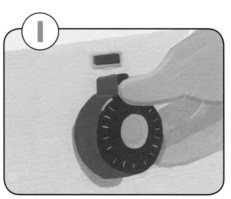

1 Preheat oven to 375°.

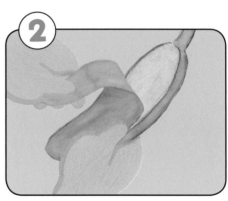

2 Remove peel from one side of a banana.

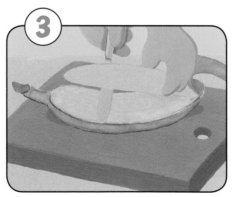

3 Use the butter knife to cut a small wedge out of the banana.

4 Place 1/4 of the marshmallows, 1/4 of the chocolate chips, and 1 teaspoon of brown sugar into the wedge of each banana.

16

NUTRITION NOTE★ Bananas are an excellent source of potassium, a mineral that helps keep your heart healthy.

5

Cover with the banana peel. Wrap each banana tightly in aluminum foil and place on a baking sheet.

6 Ask an adult to bake the wrapped bananas for 8 minutes or until the chocolate has melted. Let cool 10 minutes and serve.

This Recipe Includes
GRAINS

Cookie Decorating Party

INGREDIENTS

1/4 cup flour, for sprinkling
16 1/2-ounce package
    refrigerated sugar
    cookie dough
1 1/2 cups confectioners'
    sugar
1/4 cup milk
Food coloring, optional
Sprinkles and other cookie
    decorations

TOOLS

Measuring cups
Rolling pin
Cookie cutters
Metal spatula
2 baking sheets
Oven mitts
Small mixing bowl
Whisk
Cooling rack
Butter knife

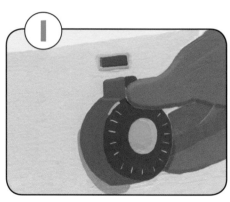

Preheat the oven to 350°.

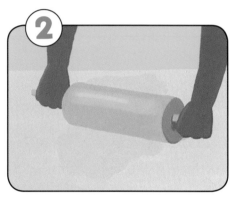

Sprinkle the counter and rolling pin with flour. Roll the dough out to 1/8 inch thickness. [NOTE: Sprinkle the dough with a little extra flour as needed to keep it from sticking to the counter and rolling pin.]

Cut the dough into shapes with cookie cutters and transfer to the baking sheets with a spatula. Combine the dough scraps into a ball, roll, and cut into shapes. Repeat with remaining dough.

Ask an adult to bake the cookies according to package directions. Transfer cookies to a cooling rack.

18

5

Pour the confectioners' sugar and milk into a small mixing bowl and whisk until combined. Add a few drops of food coloring, if desired.

6

Spread the frosting on the cooled cookies with a butter knife.

7 Top with sprinkles and other decorations and serve.

This Recipe Includes

FRUITS

Sleepover Chocolate Fondue

INGREDIENTS

2 tablespoons sugar

1 cup heavy cream

12-ounce bag semisweet
   chocolate chips

1 tablespoon butter

Assorted dippers, such as
   cut-up fruit or cubed
   angel food cake (about
   1/2 cup per serving)

TOOLS

Measuring cups

Measuring spoons

Medium microwave-safe
   bowl

Oven mitts

Whisk

Wooden skewers

NOTE: You can keep your
chocolate fondue warm with
a fondue pot, or just reheat
it in the microwave when it
cools down.

20

1

Pour the sugar, heavy cream,
chocolate chips, and butter into
a medium microwave-safe bowl
and stir.

2

Ask an adult to heat the mixture
in the microwave for 2 minutes
or until the chocolate is melted.

3

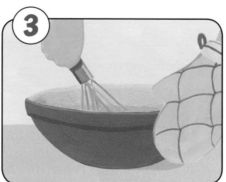

Whisk the chocolate mixture well.

4 Serve with your favorite
fruit as dippers. Use
wooden skewers to
dip the fruit.

FOOD FACT★ Fondue comes from the French
word *fonder*, which means "to melt."

21

This Recipe Includes
VEGETABLES

Sleepy Day Chicken Noodle Soup

INGREDIENTS

1 medium carrot
1 stalk of celery
1/2 teaspoon dried basil
1/2 teaspoon dried thyme
1/4 teaspoon ground pepper
1 cup water
4 cups low-sodium
    chicken broth
1 cup fine egg noodles
Crackers for serving,
    optional

TOOLS

Vegetable peeler
Small, sharp knife
Cutting board
Measuring spoons
Measuring cups
Large microwave-safe bowl
Plastic wrap
Oven mitts
Ladle

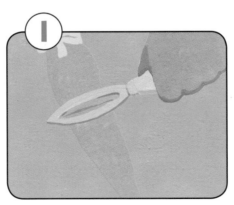
Wash the carrot. Ask an adult to peel it with a vegetable peeler and slice it.

Wash the celery and have an adult slice it.

Place the celery, carrot, basil, thyme, pepper, water, chicken broth, and noodles in a large microwave-safe bowl.

Cover the bowl tightly with plastic wrap.

5 Ask an adult to cook the soup in the microwave for 15 minutes. Let it cool for 5 minutes.

6 Scoop the soup into bowls with a ladle and serve with the crackers, if desired.

This Recipe Includes
GRAINS

Bake Sale Brownies

INGREDIENTS

3/4 cup unsalted butter

Six 1-ounce squares
 unsweetened chocolate

2 cups sugar

3 eggs

1 teaspoon pure vanilla
 extract

1 cup all-purpose flour

1 cup chopped walnuts,
 optional

TOOLS

Cooking spray

9-by-13-inch baking pan

Paring knife

Cutting board

Measuring cups

Large microwave-safe
 bowl

Wooden spoon

Measuring spoons

Rubber spatula

Oven mitts

12 small resealable
 plastic bags

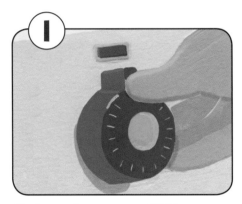

Preheat the oven to 325°.

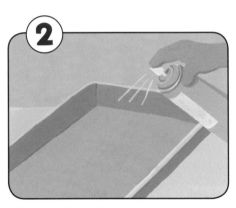

Grease the baking pan with cooking spray.

Cut the butter into small cubes. Place the chocolate and butter in a large microwave–safe bowl. Ask an adult to heat the mixture in the microwave for 2 minutes or until butter is melted. Stir until the chocolate is completely melted.

Add the sugar into the melted chocolate and stir.

24

FOOD FACT★ The seeds of the cacao tree are roasted, ground, and sweetened with sugar to make chocolate.

Add the eggs and vanilla and stir.

Add the flour and nuts and stir.

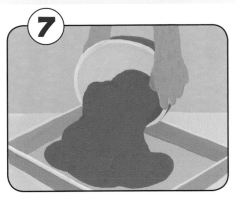

Pour the brownie batter into the baking pan and spread with a rubber spatula.

Ask an adult to bake the brownies in the oven for 30 minutes. Let the brownies cool in the pan for 30 minutes. Cut into 12 squares.

9 Place the brownies into individual bags to sell.

homemade brownies

25¢

Holiday Snowflakes

INGREDIENTS

2 tablespoons
   unsalted butter
12 wonton wrappers,
   covered with damp paper
   towels to keep moist
1 large egg
2 tablespoons
   confectioners' sugar
1 tablespoon
   granulated sugar
Pinch of salt

TOOLS

Paper towels
Parchment paper
Baking sheet
Measuring spoons
Small microwave-safe bowl
Kitchen shears
Small mixing bowl
Whisk
Pastry brush
Oven mitts
Metal spatula

26

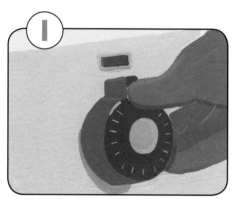

Preheat the oven to 350°.

Line the baking sheet with parchment paper. Place the butter in a small microwave-safe bowl. Ask an adult to heat the butter in the microwave for 45 seconds or until melted.

Fold one wonton wrapper in half, then fold it in half again to form a square. With the kitchen shears, cut shapes into the sides of the wrapper as you would to make a paper snowflake. Repeat with the remaining wonton wrappers.

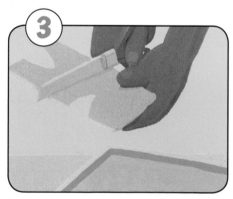

Crack the egg into a small mixing bowl and gently scoop out the yolk with your hand to leave the egg white behind. Throw the yolk away.

FOOD FACT★ Wonton wrappers are similar to pasta. In Chinese cooking, they are filled with meat or other foods to make wontons or dumplings.

5

Add the confectioners' sugar, granulated sugar, and salt to the egg white. Whisk until foamy.

6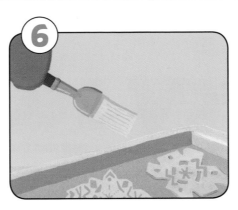

Open the wonton snowflakes. Brush each side with melted butter. Place the buttered snowflakes on the prepared baking sheet.

7

Brush the top of each snowflake with the egg white mixture. Ask an adult to bake the snowflakes in the oven for 7 minutes or until golden and crispy. Cool for 5 minutes.

8 Gently transfer the snowflakes to a plate with a spatula and serve.

27

This Recipe Includes

MILK

Rocky Road Fudge

INGREDIENTS

14-ounce can sweetened
    condensed milk
12-ounce bag semisweet
    chocolate chips
1 teaspoon vanilla extract
3 cups mini marshmallows
1 1/2 cups chopped walnuts,
    optional

TOOLS

Aluminum foil
8-by-8-inch baking pan
Cooking spray
Can opener
Medium microwave-safe
    bowl
Oven mitts
Rubber spatula
Measuring spoons
Measuring cups
Plastic wrap
Cutting board
Small, sharp knife

1

Line the baking pan with aluminum foil, letting some foil hang over the sides. Grease the foil-lined pan with cooking spray.

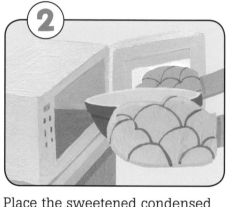

2

Place the sweetened condensed milk and chocolate chips in a medium microwave-safe bowl. Ask an adult to heat the mixture in the microwave for 90 seconds or until the chocolate is softened.

3

Stir the mixture with a rubber spatula until smooth.

4

Add the vanilla extract, marshmallows, and walnuts (optional) to the chocolate mixture and stir.

NUTRITION NOTE★ Walnuts contain omega-3 fatty acids, which help keep your heart healthy.

5 Scrape the mixture into the baking pan and spread it evenly. Cover the pan with plastic wrap and chill in the refrigerator for 1 hour or until firm.

6 Remove the plastic wrap. Lift the foil to remove the fudge and flip it over onto a cutting board.

7 Peel away the foil and cut the fudge into squares.

This Recipe Includes

GRAINS, MILK

Happy Birthday Cupcakes

INGREDIENTS
1 1/4 cups all-purpose flour
1/3 cup unsweetened
   cocoa powder
1 1/2 teaspoons baking
   soda
1/8 teaspoon salt
1/2 cup unsalted butter,
   room temperature
1 cup sugar
1 large egg
1 cup milk
1 teaspoon pure
   vanilla extract
1 teaspoon balsamic
   vinegar

TOOLS
2 muffin tins
Muffin cups
Measuring cups
Measuring spoons
Medium mixing bowl
Wooden spoon
Large mixing bowl
Fork
Spoon
Rubber spatula
Oven mitts
Toothpick

Preheat the oven to 350°.

Line muffin tins with muffin cups.

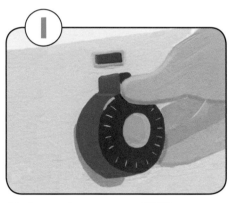

Pour the flour, cocoa powder, baking soda, and salt into a medium mixing bowl and stir.

Place the butter and sugar into a large mixing bowl and mash with a fork until combined.

30

Add the egg, milk, and vanilla to the butter mixture and beat with a wooden spoon until no big lumps remain.

Add the flour mixture a few spoonfuls at a time and stir with a rubber spatula until smooth.

Add the vinegar and stir until the batter is smooth.

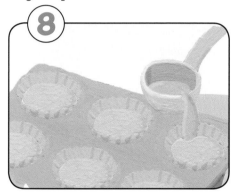

Spoon the batter into the muffin cups, filling them about three-quarters full.

Ask an adult to bake the cupcakes in the oven for 25 minutes, or until a toothpick inserted into the center comes out clean. Let the cupcakes cool in the pan.

10   Serve.

31

INDEX

ON THE WEB

FactHound offers a safe, fun way to find Web sites related to topics in this book. All of the sites on FactHound have been researched by our staff.

1. Visit *www.facthound.com*
2. Type in this special code: 1404840001
3. Click on the FETCH IT button.

Your trusty FactHound will fetch the best sites for you!

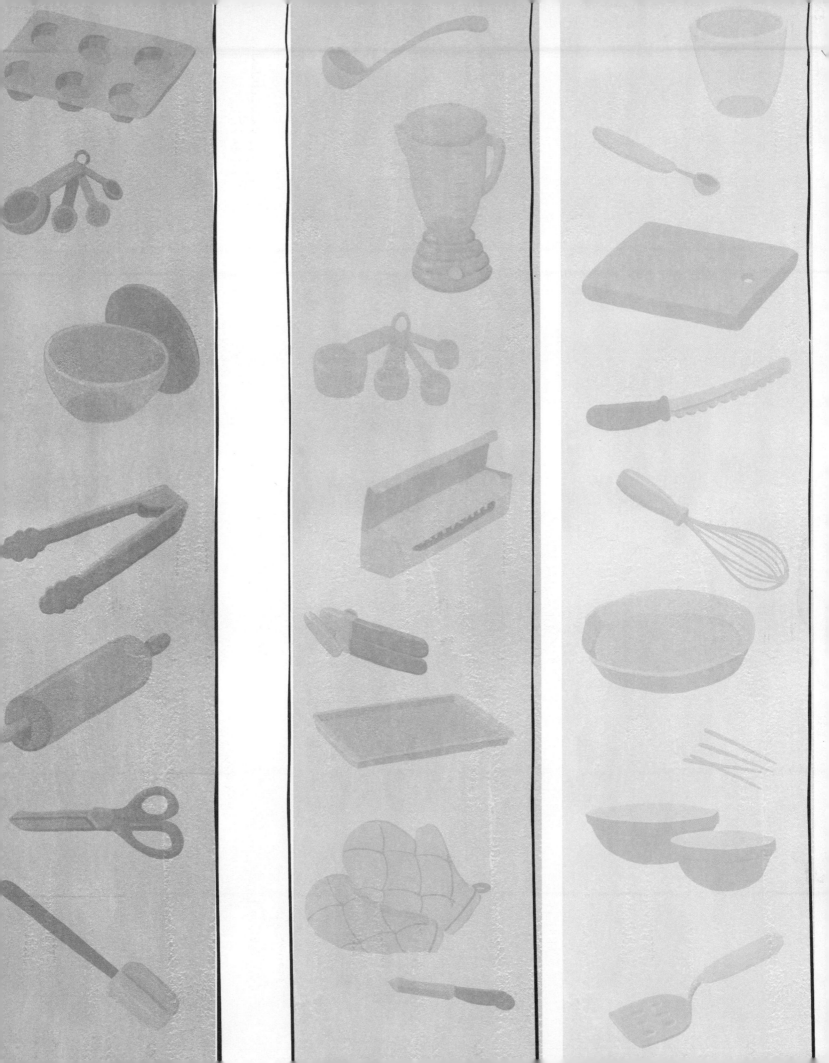

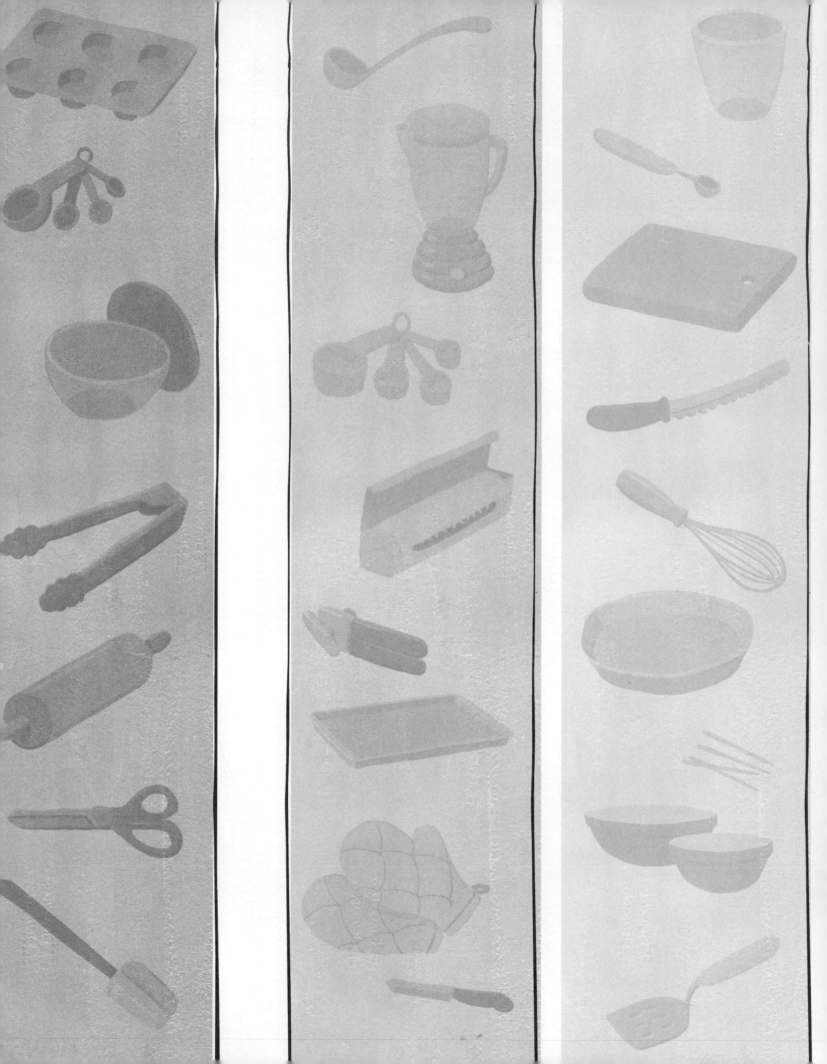